1

I WALK IN FAVOR

31 -DAY Devotional Affirmations And Inspirations
For Women

ISBN :978-1-948971-03-4

Written and Designed by Damola Treasure Okenla

Published By

HILLTOP CREATIVE PUBLISHERS- USA

HILLTOP
Creative Publishers
PUSHING OUT THE MESSAGE FROM WITHIN

This Book Is A Gift

From:

_____

To:

_____

Date:

_____

WHAT ABOUT FAVOR?

Jesus increased in favor, Mary had favor in bring Him to the world, Noah found favor, Esther received favor, Ruth looked forward to favoring and got it, Joseph received favor in a foreign land, and king Saul received favor from strangers. So what is favor, and why do you need as a treasured woman? Favor is a special privilege granted to an individual to be exceptionally treated above others. You can call it a supernatural fragrance or charm that sets one apart from others. Favor attracts unsolicited good and more essential things from the known and unknown. I call it a supernatural appeal! It is magnetic, and as a treasured woman, you don't have a choice but to wear it. In this book, you will find something to muse on to walk in favor every time, everywhere, and with everyone.

Luke 2:52; Luke 1:30; Genesis 6:8;Ruth 2:2,10; Genesis 39;1 Samuel 10

HALL OF FAME

TREASURED WOMEN WHO FOUND AND WALKED IN FAVOR FAVOR

RUTH: A book was dedicated to this treasured woman, who was a Moabite widow from a cursed tribe but found herself in the genealogy of Jesus Christ. She went in search of favor, and she got it. Her story can be found in the book of Ruth, from Chapter one to chapter four

Esther: She started as a foreign slave and ended up becoming the Queen to the most powerful monarch of her time and not just that; by extension of favor bestowed upon her, she was able to save the Jewish from going into extinction. Her story is found in the book, Esther chapter one to chapter ten.

MARY: The young girl who had favor entrusted upon her to carry and bring forth our Lord Jesus Christ. Her story can found in the book Luke chapteR one.

YOU :(PLEASE INSERT YOUR NAME)

FAVOR : WHAT IT IS

Favor is an attitude of approval or liking.
_Esther 2:17; Genesis 39:21-23;Acts 7: 9-
10,45-46

Favor is an act of kindness beyond what
is due.

Favor is a special privilege or status that
is granted to a person.
_ 2 Corinthians 6:2

Favor is a supernatural fragrance that attracts unsolicited help or kindness.
_Acts 2: 46 -47

Favor overturn curses to blessings. Ruth was a woman who had everything against her, but by favor, she got into the lineage of our Lord Jesus Christ.
_Psalm 126:1-6; 30:5; 85:1

Favor is a special privilege or status that is granted to a person.

THE POWER OF FAVOR

- The favor of God will supersede anything that may have ever happened to you or anything you may have done wrong.

- The mercy and favor of God will deliver to you the unexpected and undeserved blessings.-1 Samuel 2:8; 2 Samuel 9:8

- Favor will supernaturally provide. promote, protect, and preserve you. _ Numbers 6:24 -26; Leviticus 26:9

  - The favor of God will turn the opposition to opportunity and turn your adversaries to your supporters. _ Exodus 3:21; 11:3 ; 12:36 ; Daniel 3:30

- Favor will make you or your products noticeable and desirable even in an obscure place. _Genesis 4:4

- Favor will bring you into fulfillment and increase. _ Genesis 6:8; 18: 3-5

THE POWER OF FAVOR

- Favor will add beauty to your life and make your destiny colorful.

- Favor qualifies the unqualified and terminates judgment against a favored person .

- Favor will single you out for spectacular breakthroughs and unusual encounters.

- Favor will set you ahead of the line; It does not matter how many people have gone ahead or how far they have gone.

- Favor will attract help to you from unusual places and people.

- Favor will make you outstanding, extraordinary, distinguished, and exceptional. _Exodus 33:12 -13

THE POWER OF FAVOR

- Favor makes you unique and endearing to others. _Luke 2:52

- Favor is a magnet for good and great things.

- To be favored is to be preferred above others.

- Favor is a seasoning; it adds flavor to your labor.

- Favor is a tool of deliverance from the pit of despair (1 Samuel 2:8)

- Favor is a limit and barrier breaker (2Samuel 9:8)

THE POWER OF FAVOR

- Favor brings restoration of lifetime losses (2 Sam. 9; PS.30:5)

- Favor is an impenetrable shield builder (Ps.5:12)

- Favor turns opposition to promotion (Daniel 3:30; Esther 9)

- Favor will set a person ahead of the line (PS.47:3 MSG)

- Favor Is a ladder for the supernatural elevation (Genesis 39: 2-4, 21-23;41 38-40)
- Favor is a continuous experience in God and not a one-time thing (Luke 2:52)

- Favor is a seed to a mighty harvest, that is you sow it, and you reap it.

- Favor of God upon your life will continue to increase as you regularly declare it with your mouth (Proverbs 18:21)

But my horn (emblem of excessive strength and stately grace) You have exalted like that of a wild ox; I am anointed with fresh oil.

PSALM 92:10

The Lord God is like the sun that gives us light. He is like a shield that keeps us safe.   The Lord blesses us with favor and honor.He doesn't hold back anything good from those whose lives are without blame.

PSALM 84:11

Now the boy Samuel grew and was in favor both with the Lord and with men.

1 SAMUEL 2:26

I am grateful to my heavenly Father for the past, both the good and the ugly; I am blessed and highly favored. Consequently, all things are working together for me.

My Heavenly Father by favor shall break every protocol of heaven and earth. He will do the unexplainable, unprecedented, and inexplicable in my life and destiny that His name only, will be glorified.

By favor, my mess is whirling to a divine message and my frustration to divine fulfillment.

I AM A WOMAN. I AM A TREASURE!

It is my season of divine visitation for a drastic, dramatic and dimensional turn-around and breakthroughs.

I AM A WOMAN. I AM A TREASURE!

By favor, my pain has turn to pleasure and my lamentation to laughter. By favor instead of troubles, I have testimonies, and my pains are converting to profits.

By favor, my night has turned to morning, my problems resulting in promotion and disappointment to divine appointment.

I believe the favor of God on my life is not for me to keep to myself and become proud of, but to be used for others.

LUKE BENWARD

Add favor to the list of your favorite perfumes and daily sprinkle a dash of it.

DAMOLA TREASURE OKENLA

Your situation may look impossible, but don't ever rule out the favor of God.

JOEL OSTEEN

*And Ruth the Moabitess said to Naomi,
Let me go to the field and glean among
the ears of grain after him in whose sight
I shall find favor. Naomi said to her, Go,
my daughter.*

RUTH 2:2

*But the Lord God keeps me   from being
disgraced.So I refuse to give up,because I
know   God will never let me down. My
protector is nearby;no one can stand here   to
accuse me of wrong. The Lord God will help
me   and prove I am innocent.My accusers will
wear out   like moth-eaten clothes.*

ISAIAH 50:7-9

I AM A WOMAN. I AM A TREASURE!

By favor, my weakness has become my strength. Every curse hanging over my destiny has turned to a blessing. My trouble has turned to testimony.

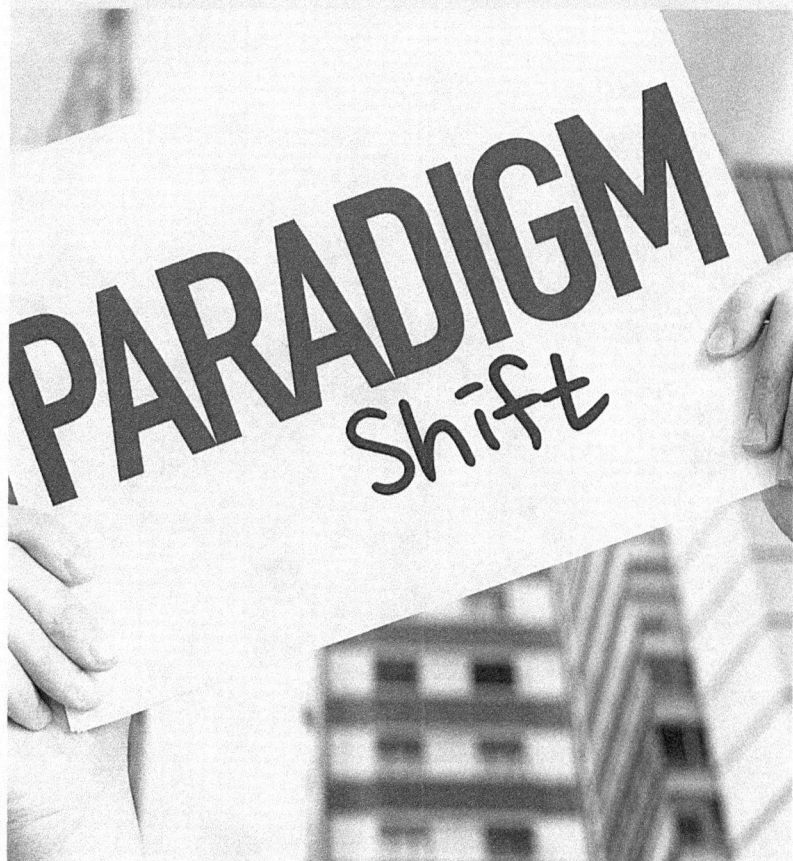

By favor, I shall not wander into parched places; but I shall always be at the right place at the right time, and only the right people will take notice of me.

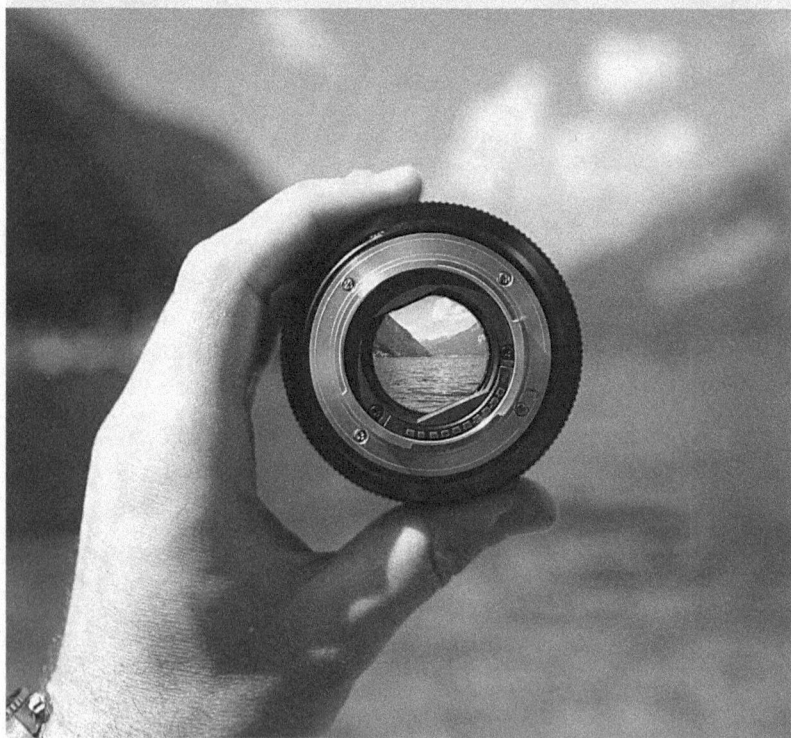

By favor, my life shall no longer be a candidate for error and missteps. The power of failure and mistake can no longer function in my life. I have received the spirit of good judgment, accuracy, and precision.

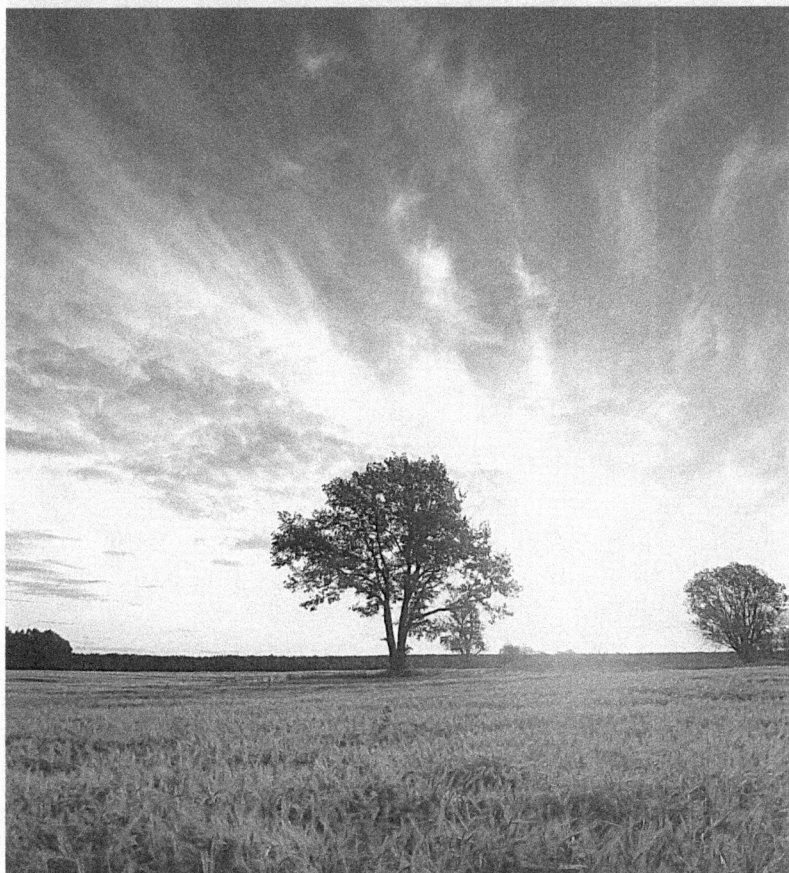

I AM A WOMAN. I AM A TREASURE!

By favor, I operate in the spirit of wisdom and understanding for accurate evaluations of people, places, and problems.

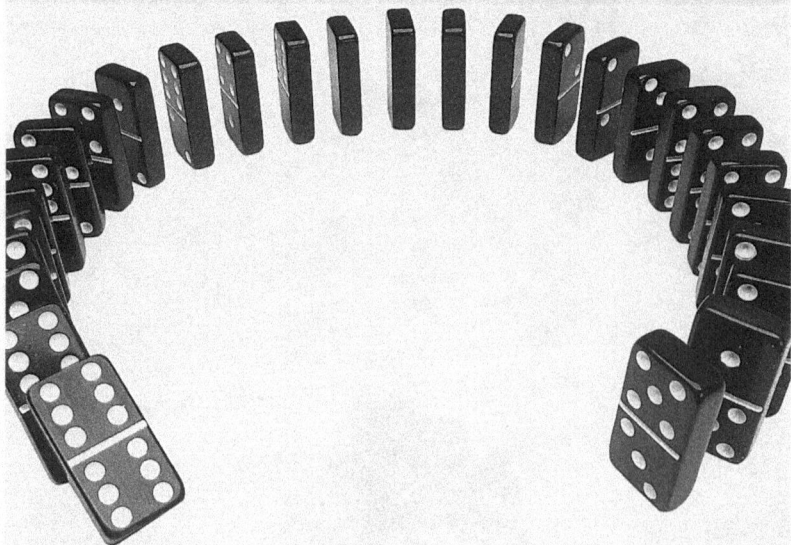

By favor, my feet have been made beautiful, and it has become an agent of good news and useful reports. My legs are leading me to where destiny is awaiting me.

Then she fell on her face, bowing to the ground, and said to him, Why have I found favor in your eyes that you should notice me, when I am a foreigner?

RUTH 2:10

I've learned that his anger lasts for a moment,but his loving favor lasts a lifetime![a]We may weep through the night,but at daybreak it will turn into shouts of ecstatic joy.

PSALM 30:5

And the angel said to her, Do not be afraid, Mary, for you have found grace ([a]free, spontaneous, absolute favor and loving-kindness) with God.

LUKE 1:30

> 99

When God grants you His favor, nothing can stop the blessings He has in store.

ANNETTA POWELL

Sow a seed of favor into someone else's life to reap a harvest of favor.

DAMOLA TREASURE OKENLA

When God has selected you, it doesn't matter who has rejected or neglected you. God's favor outweighs all opposition.

ANONYMOUS

I am a child of destiny, and by God's favor, I shall get to my destination regardless of the odds against me. By God's grace, I shall not perish in the wilderness of life, but I shall come out into a season of fruitfulness and abundance in the mighty name of Jesus. I am blessed and highly favored.

I AM A WOMAN. I AM A TREASURE!

I am receiving favor and compassion in the sight of all men; my ordained helpers are rising to favor me.

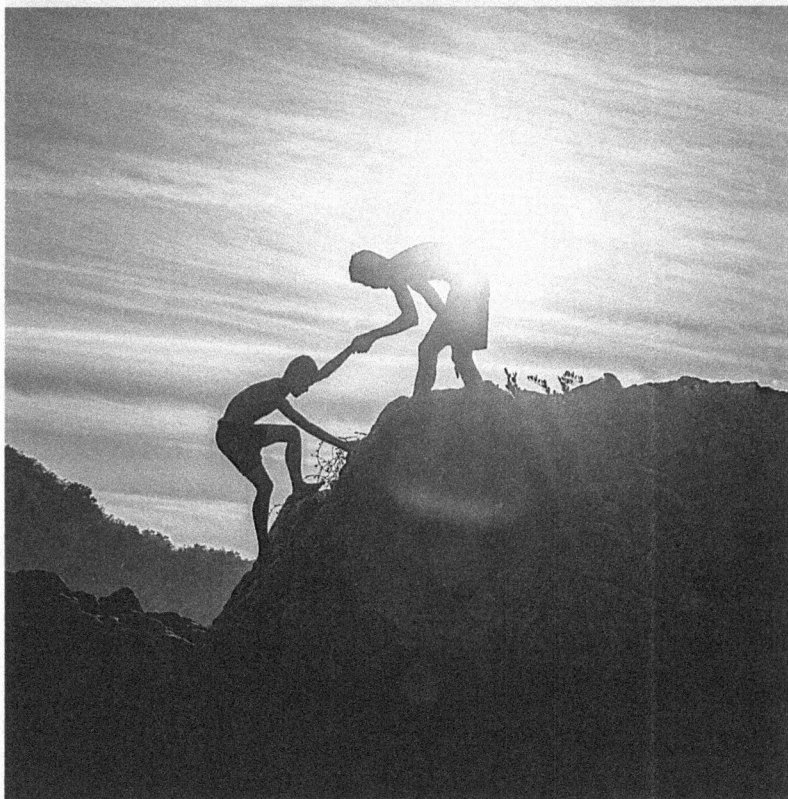

In my business, ministry, and career, I am receiving favor from all associates, partners, clients, superiors, and subordinates. By inclination, men of influence will speak for me and to me. I am receiving endorsements; from every angle from men and women who can advance my cause in life.

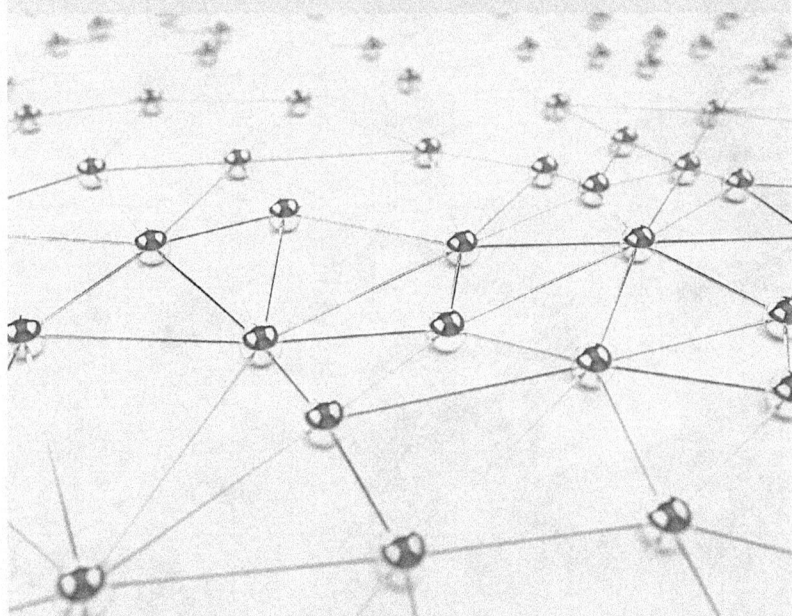

By favor, I am strategically positioned for higher and better things yet to come.

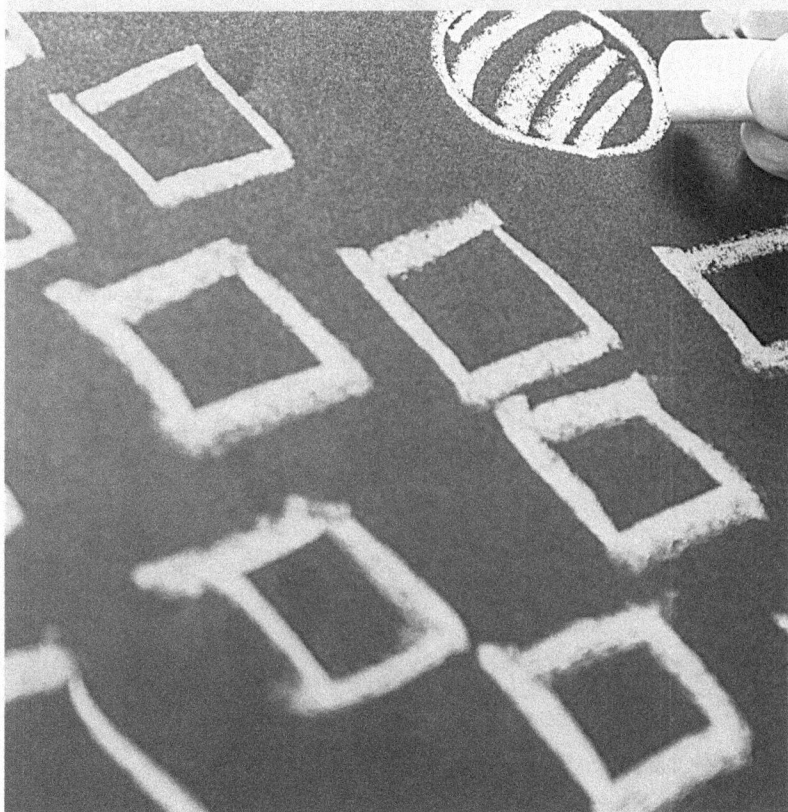

By favor, my adversity is turning to a stepping stone for my advancement. I walk in victory over every adversity,

But the Lord was with Joseph, and showed him mercy and loving-kindness and gave him favor in the sight of the warden of the prison. And the warden of the prison committed to Joseph's care all the prisoners who were in the prison; and whatsoever was done there, he was in charge of it.

GENESIS 39 : 21 - 22

When the turn came for Esther (the young woman Mordecai had adopted, the daughter of his uncle Abihail) to go to the king, she asked for nothing other than what Hegai, the king's eunuch who was in charge of the harem, suggested. And Esther won the favor of everyone who saw her. She was taken to King Xerxes in the royal residence in the tenth month, the month of Tebeth, in the seventh year of his reign.

ESTHER 2:15-16

The safest place to be is still under the shadow of the ALMIGHTY; Are you there yet?

DAMOLA TREASURE OKENLA

Hangout with God, and you will continue to increase in favor with men.

DAMOLA TREASURE OKENLA

For Peter to become a wonder he had to surrender his boat; What are you holding back? You can surrender it now, to gain the favor that will turns things around for you.

DAMOLA TREASURE OKENLA

I AM A WOMAN. I AM A TREASURE!

By favor, something distinctive and dramatic is about to happen in my life, something that no eyes have discovered or any ear have deduced.

I AM A WOMAN. I AM A TREASURE!

By favor, my designated moment is now! From henceforth, all eyes that see me will favor me; all tongue shall proclaim me blessed.

By favor, everything that I have lost is coming back to me - blessings, privileges, honor, dignity, promotion, resources, connections, and inheritance.

I am receiving favor from the decision-makers in any matter that relates to me.

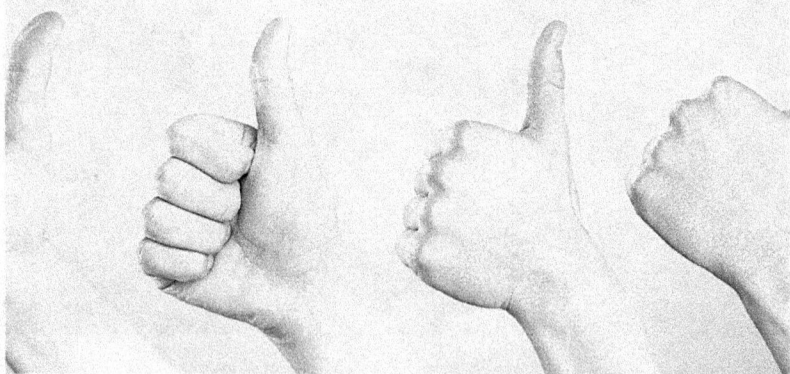

By favor, my proposals are receiving rapid approvals, no resentment, no rejection.

Now the king was attracted to Esther more than to any of the other women, and she won his favor and approval more than any of the other virgins. So he set a royal crown on her head and made her queen instead of Vashti.

ESTHER 2:17

You will arise and have compassion on Zion,   for it is time to show favor to her;   the appointed time has come.

PSALM 102:13

And Jesus increased in wisdom (in broad and full understanding) and in stature and years, and in favor with God and man.

LUKE 2:52

I AM A WOMAN. I AM A TREASURE!

Favor is connecting me to the right men and women who are influential in the fulfillment of my dreams and destiny.

> Someone else may have more talent, connection, education, experience or exposure but God's favor will cause you get to a destination that you cannot get to by yourself.

DAMOLA TREASURE OKENLA

> It's your season! Your trials are turning to testimonies, and your pain is being converted to gain.

DAMOLA TREASURE OKENLA

> Men and women of old who walked in enormous favor were intimate with God. Determine to pursue God and walk intimately with Him.

DAMOLA TREASURE OKENLA

I am wonderfully blessed with the favor of God wrapped around me like a shield to protect me from all assaults, and known and unknown danger. I am excluded from any imminent destruction.

By favor, I am experiencing acceptance instead of rejection. I reject fear of rejection; men and women have no choice but to accept me.

I AM A WOMAN. I AM A TREASURE!

The favor of God upon my life will only magnetize to me, men and women who will appreciate and value my potentials, and not time wasters or anyone who will devalue my worth.

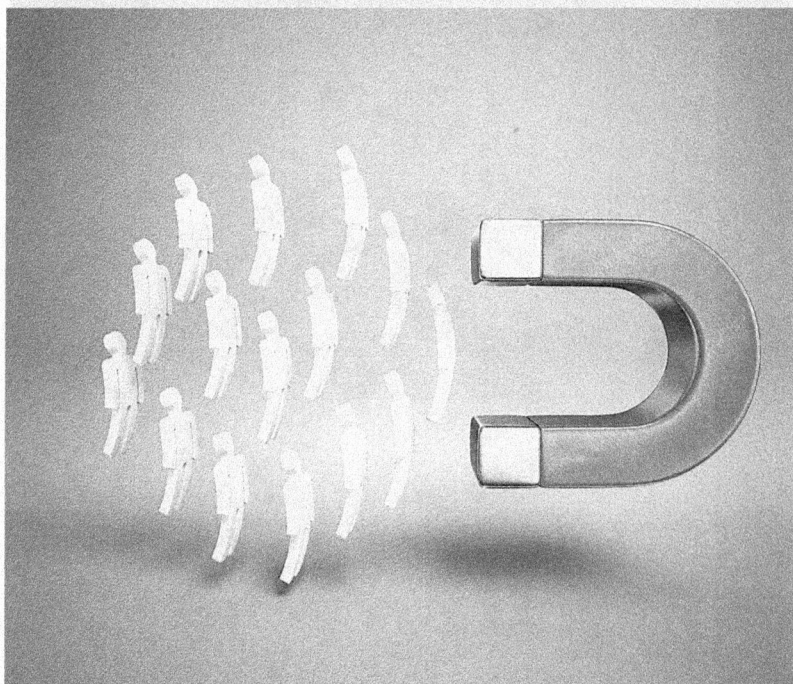

As I continue to walk in humility, the favor will expose me to those with the capacity to help me.

And the maiden pleased [Hegai] and obtained his favor. And he speedily gave her the things for her purification and her portion of food and the seven chosen maids to be given her from the king's palace; and he removed her and her maids to the best [apartment] in the harem.

ESTHER 2:9

But Noah found grace (favor) in the eyes of the Lord.

GENESIS 6:8

So Joseph pleased [Potiphar] and found favor in his sight, and he served him. And [his master] made him supervisor over his house and he put all that he had in his charge.

GENESIS 39 : 4

"

Are you going through any adverse situation? Look through, for any opportunity to advance your destiny.

DAMOLA TREASURE OKENLA

Storms are not meant to destroy you, but to toughen you.

DAMOLA TREASURE OKENLA

Do not be afraid of competition and competitors; prepare yourself excellently and diligently and believe God for the best.

DAMOLA TREASURE OKENLA

I am walking in enormous favor, and by inclination, I am a magnet to good and great things

Favor is beautifying my life with wonders. By favor, I'm distinguished for exploits and greatness in all spheres.

By favor, I am entering into a season of restoration and recovery; I'm recovering everything vital-tangible and intangible.

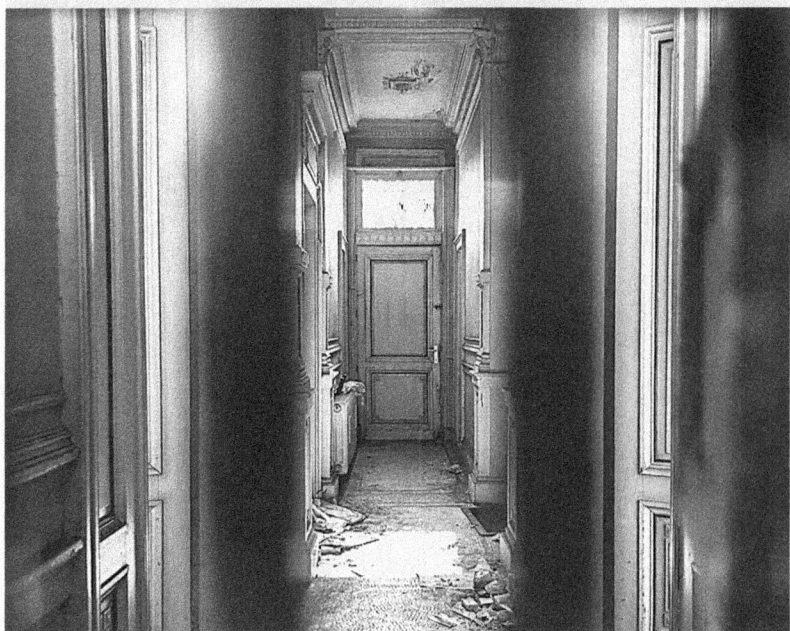

I AM A WOMAN. I AM A TREASURE!

By favor, I am singled out for Divine intervention and the season of endless struggles and stagnancy is terminated over my life.

I AM A WOMAN. I AM A TREASURE!

My life is perfumed with the fragrance of favor. It's connecting me with true love, kindness and help.

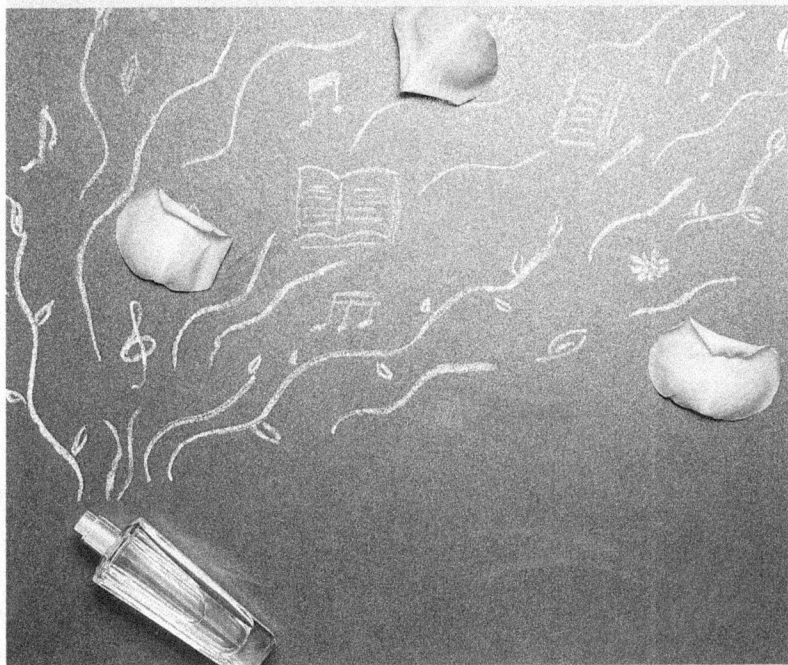

I AM A WOMAN. I AM A TREASURE!

My labor has the flavor of favor for worthy rewards.

And when the king saw Esther the queen standing in the court, she obtained favor in his sight, and he held out to [her] the golden scepter that was in his hand. So Esther drew near and touched the tip of the scepter.

ESTHER 5 : 2

Lord, how wonderfully you bless the righteous.Your favor wraps around each one and covers themunder your canopy of kindness and joy.

PSALM 5:12

But in the depths of my heart I truly knowthat you, Yahweh, have become my Shield;You take me and surround me with yourself.[a]Your glory covers me continually.[b]You lift high my head when I bow low in shame.

PSALM 3:3

I AM A WOMAN. I AM A TREASURE!

I have the anointing of favor upon my life, and my head shall not run dry of the oil of gladnesss, in Jesus' name.

I AM A WOMAN. I AM A TREASURE!

I am a child of God. I am blessed and highly favored. I live by favor; I work and walk-in favor. I have favor with God and with men. My favor shall not turn to disfavor. My grace shall not turn to disgrace.

Excellence is favor multiplier. What is your excellence rate? You can increase your favor by increasing your level of excellence where you most need a favor.

DAMOLA TREASURE OKENLA

Imagine what difference you can make where you are and start to working on it.

DAMOLA TREASURE OKENLA

Your efforts without divine input could be at best produce frustrations. Ensure you Involve divinity in all your labor efforts.

DAMOLA TREASURE OKENLA

The glory of your splendor is our strength,and your marvelous favor makes us even stronger,lifting us even higher!

PSALM 89:17

Wash and anoint yourself therefore, and put on your best clothes and go down to the threshing floor, but do not make yourself known to the man until he has finished eating and drinking.

RUTH 3:3

Each young woman's turn came to go in to King Ahasuerus after she had completed twelve months' preparation, according to the regulations for the women, for thus were the days of their preparation apportioned: six months with oil of myrrh, and six months with perfumes and preparations for beautifying women.

ESTHER 2:12

ACTIVATION

Desire it and ask for it!
Matthew 7:7-11

ACTIVATION

Make Your Way Pleasing To The Lord
Proverbs 16:7

ACTIVATION

Surround yourself with wise people
Psalm 1; Proverbs 12:15; Proverbs 11:14

CAUTION

Unfortunately, if you can find a favor, you can lose it. The person that gives you favor can also take it from you. Someone can confer a favor on you as well as remove it. So treasure and guard it jealously.
_Esther 1:12,19; proverbs 13:15

ACTIVATION

Favor increases with the right association.

ACTIVATION

Favor multiplies by declaring it with your mouth

Proverbs 18:21

ACTIVATION

You have to perceive it to conceive it. When you imagine, you believe and accept it

CAUTION

Obedience is a catalyst to receive godly favor.

Likewise, disobedience is a minus.

Isaiah 1:19; Job 36:11

ACTIVATION

As you boost your level of excellence, so also your level of favor increases.

Daniel 5:12;6:2

ACTIVATION

Daily as you spray on your perfume, don't forget your spiritual fragrance.

Ruth 3:3;Ps. 45:8;Esther 2:12;Ezekiel 16:9;Luke 7:38,46;7:17; Proverbs 27:9;1 Peter 3:3-4

Are you visible and available for help? Drop the ego and make yourself visible and accessible for support; You never know how God will work things out in your favor and who He hasdesignated for that purpose.

DAMOLA TREASURE OKENLA

Determine to offer to your clients the best product and service and commit your projects and products to God and hope for the best.

DAMOLA TREASURE OKENLA

Regardless of your current situation, determine not to give up, and favor will see you through.

DAMOLA TREASURE OKENLA

LET'S CONNECT

FACEBOOK
https://www.facebook.com/iamatreasuredwoman/

PINTEREST
https://www.pinterest.com/treasuredwoman1/

INSTAGRAM
https://www.instagram.com/iamatreasuredwoman/

HILLTOP
Creative Publishers
PUSHING OUT THE MESSAGE FROM WITHIN

CONTACT US

For Orders and Inquiries

EMAIL ADDRESS
Treasuredwoman1@gmail.com

PHONE NUMBER
(708)5403090

WWW.IAMATREASUREDWOMAN.COM

BOOKS BY DAMOLA

DAMOLA TREASURE OKENLA

As an award-winning author of several Christian books and a highly sought-after inspirational speaker, Damola Treasure Okenla is dedicated to uplifting others mentally, spiritually, and emotionally. For more than ten years, she has partnered with individuals and groups to inspire and motivate others to live the life God intended for them to live—assisting them in rebuilding and recovering from losses and setbacks in life. As the president and founder of Life Encounters, Inc., a non-profit organization that is dedicated to self-discovery and recovery, Damola facilitates seminars, workshops, and retreats to usher others into purpose fulfillment. Her organization, like her books, is a small reflection of her passion and mission for the advocacy of spiritual freedom and empowerment. Damola serves as the president and founder of Hilltop Publishing, where she assists Christian authors with publishing and social media management for their book projects—positioning them for excellence in the marketplace. Apart from ministry, Damola works as an accountant and project manager and holds a Master's in Public Administration. More than anything, Damola is on a mission to help others discover their true potential, live a life of purpose, and earn a profit while doing it. For more information or bookings, visit www.damolatreasureokenla.com or call 800.767.0728.

www.ingramcontent.com/pod-product-compliance
Lightning Source LLC
Chambersburg PA
CBHW060535030426
42337CB00021B/4282